STEM *trailblazer* BIOS

MATHEMATICIAN AND COMPUTER SCIENTIST
GRACE HOPPER

ANDREA PELLESCHI

Lerner Publications ◆ Minneapolis

Lerner Publications Company
A division of Lerner Publishing Group, Inc.
241 First Avenue North
Minneapolis, MN 55401 U.S.A.

For reading levels and more information, look up this title at www.lernerbooks.com.

Content Consultant: Dr. C. Dianne Martin, Professor, Computer Science Department, George Washington University

Library of Congress Cataloging-in-Publication Data

Names: Pelleschi, Andrea, 1962– author.
Title: Mathematician and computer scientist Grace Hopper / Andrea Pelleschi.
Description: Minneapolis : Lerner Publications, [2016] | Series: STEM trailblazer bios | Includes
    bibliographical references and index. | Audience: Ages 7–11.
Identifiers: LCCN 2016006145 (print) | LCCN 2016006401 (ebook) | ISBN 9781512407853 (lb : alk.
    paper) | ISBN 9781512413083 (pb : alk. paper) | ISBN 9781512410884 (eb pdf)
Subjects: LCSH: Hopper, Grace Murray—Juvenile literature. | Admirals—United States—Biography—
    Juvenile literature. | Women admirals—United States—Biography—Juvenile literature. | Computer
    engineers—United States—Biography—Juvenile literature. | Women computer engineers—United
    States—Biography—Juvenile literature.
Classification: LCC V63.H66 P45 2016 (print) | LCC V63.H66 (ebook) | DDC 004.092—dc23

LC record available at http://lccn.loc.gov/2016006145

Manufactured in the United States of America
1 – PC – 7/15/16

The images in this book are used with the permission of: © jorgecachoh/iStock/Thinkstock, 4;
Bain News Service/Library of Congress, 5; © Jonathan Feinstein/Shutterstock.com, 6; US Navy,
8, 26; © Science Source, 10, 14, 15, 21, 23; © HUP-SF Computers (2), olvwork286536, Harvard
University Archives, 11; Naval Surface Warfare Center/US Naval History and Heritage Command,
13; © AP Images, 16; © Everett Collection/Newscom, 18, 24; © Richard B. Levine/Newscom, 20;
Pete Souza/US Navy, 27; PH2 Michael Flynn/US Navy, 28.

Front Cover: US Navy.

CONTENTS

Old-fashioned alarm clocks contained many gears, which made it hard for Grace to put her alarm clocks back together after she took them apart.

A LOVE OF
LEARNING

Grace Murray was always fascinated by how things worked. When she was just seven years old, she took apart her alarm clock. She wanted to know what made the clock ring. But when she unscrewed the back plate, gears and

springs fell out. Grace did not know how to put them back together. Luckily, she had another alarm clock. She could open it and see where all the gears went. But this one had the same problem. As soon as she opened the back, everything fell out. Grace opened five more alarm clocks. The same thing happened each time.

When Grace's parents discovered the clocks, they did not scold her. They encouraged her love of learning. In fact, her mother let her have one alarm clock just so she could experiment on it.

Born in 1906, Grace was raised differently from most girls of the time. She didn't like playing with dolls or tea sets.

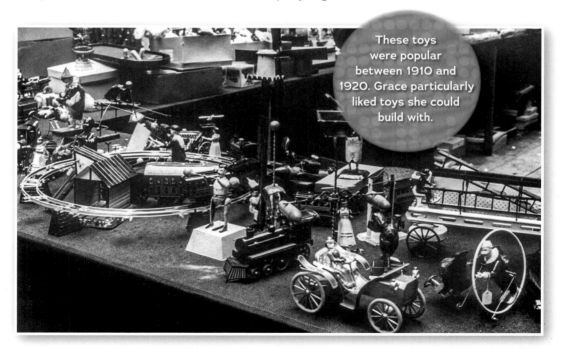

These toys were popular between 1910 and 1920. Grace particularly liked toys she could build with.

Instead, she loved building things. One of her favorite toys was a Struktiron construction kit. It was a collection of movable parts, motors, and metal pieces. Her parents encouraged her love of math and science. Grace's father believed his daughters should have every opportunity that boys had.

SCHOOL LIFE

Grace graduated from high school when she was only sixteen years old. She applied to Vassar College so she could study

Vassar College was founded in 1861 as a college for women.

math. Unfortunately, she failed the Latin portion of the entrance exam. But this did not stop her. She went to a college prep school to learn Latin. She passed the test one year later.

In 1928 Grace graduated from Vassar with a bachelor's degree in mathematics and physics. She went on to Yale University to obtain a master's degree in mathematics. The same year she completed her master's, she got married and changed her name to Grace Hopper. Then Vassar asked her to take a teaching job. She accepted. She taught a wide range of math classes, such as algebra, calculus, and statistics. While she was teaching, she continued studying at Yale. In 1934 she received a doctorate in mathematics.

TECH TALK

"I would explain [to my students], it was no use trying to learn math unless they could communicate it with other people."

—Grace Hopper, on requiring her math students at Vassar College to write essays

On December 7, 1941, the Japanese navy bombed US ships in Pearl Harbor, Hawaii. The attack drew the United States into World War II.

THE MARK COMPUTERS

The United States entered World War II in December 1941. In 1943, Hopper joined the WAVES, which stood for Women Accepted for Volunteer Emergency Service. This was an all-female unit in the US Naval Reserve. A year later,

Hopper graduated at the top of her navy class as a lieutenant junior grade.

THE MARK I

Because of Hopper's background in mathematics, the navy ordered her to report to Harvard University. Her job was to work on the first automatic digital calculator in the United States. The machine was called the Mark I. It took up an entire room in the basement of a laboratory. It was 51 feet (15.5 meters) long by 8 feet (2.4 m) high. It weighed more than 5 tons (4.5 metric tons) and housed approximately 530 miles (850 kilometers) of wire. Instead of a keyboard or mouse, the Mark I had a set of switches and relays similar to those used on dial telephones. It read instructions from a long piece of paper tape with holes punched into it. The holes in the tape

TECH TALK

"There was this large mass of machinery out there making a lot of racket. It was all bare, all open, and very noisy."

—*Grace Hopper, on seeing the Mark I for the first time*

told the machine what calculations to perform. The navy used the Mark I to compute firing distances for the big guns on ships.

When Hopper first saw the Mark I, she wanted to take it apart and study every component, just as she had with the alarm clocks. Instead, she examined blueprints of the machine. She also worked with another officer who had more experience than she did. Together, they studied how to create a **program** for the Mark I. For instance, Hopper might want to

Hopper created computer programs by punching instructions into long pieces of paper tape.

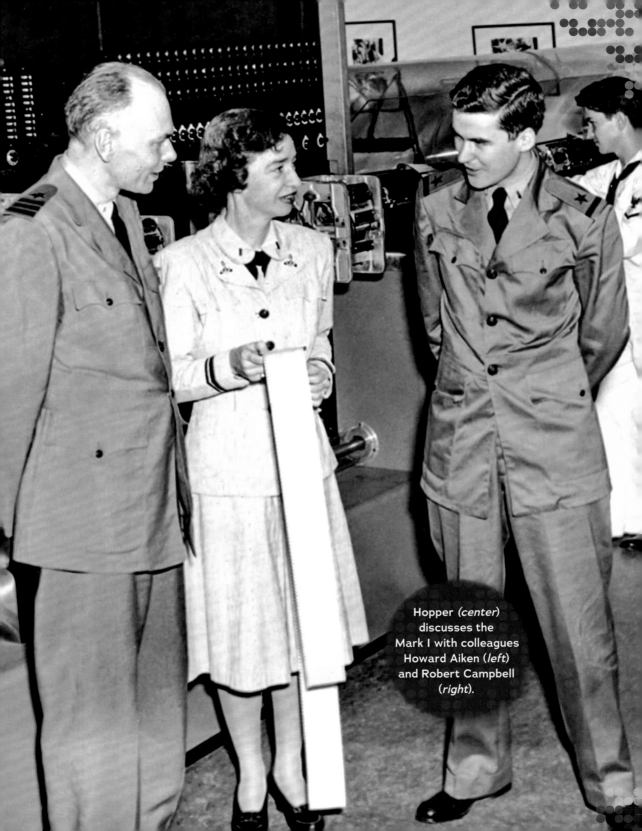

Hopper *(center)* discusses the Mark I with colleagues Howard Aiken *(left)* and Robert Campbell *(right)*.

add two numbers and then multiply them by a third number. To do that, she looked at the mathematical equation and broke it down into small steps. Then she punched the instructions into a paper tape to tell the computer what to calculate. These instructions were called a program.

Hopper and her assistants took extensive notes on how they monitored and programmed the computer. After the war, Hopper was asked to use her notes to write a book about the Mark I. The book was published in 1946 as the world's first computer manual.

In 1946, Hopper was promoted to lieutenant. Now that the war was over, she wanted to transfer to the regular navy. But, at age thirty-nine, she found out she was too old to do so. So she stayed in the naval reserve and continued to work at Harvard for three more years. During that time, she worked on the faster Mark II and Mark III computers. Each improved upon the design of the Mark I.

DEBUGGING

Over the years, many computer scientists have used the word *bug* to describe a problem in a computer. But Hopper and her colleagues were the first to discover an actual bug causing problems in their machine. One day, after the Mark II

0800   antan started
1000   "   stopped   - antan ✓   { 1.2700   9.037 847
        13″ uc (032) MP - MC   9.037 846 ?
        (033)   PRO. 2   2.130476415 4.61592
                 conect   2.130676415
        Relays 6-2 in 033 failed special speed test
        In teloy   "   11.000 test .
              Relays changed

100   Started   Cosine Tape   (Sine check)
1525   Started   Mult + Adder Test.

1545   Relay #70 Panel F
                                        (moth) in relay.

       First actual case of bug being found.
1630   antangut started.
1700   closed down .

The moth that was found trapped in the Mark II is now preserved at the National Museum of American History.

stopped working, the operator discovered that a moth had flown in through an open window. It got smashed inside the Mark II. After removing the moth, the operator taped it into the logbook and labeled it as the first actual case of a bug being found. Today, when computer scientists are trying to solve a problem, they say they are **debugging** it.

Chapter 3

Movers deliver a UNIVAC I to a University of California lab in January 1953.

A COMPUTER
REVOLUTION

In 1949, Hopper left Harvard University to join the Eckert-Mauchly Computer Corporation as a senior mathematician. Eckert-Mauchly was a private company. It had a new computer called the UNIVAC, which stood for Universal

Automatic Computer. This large-scale electronic digital computer used vacuum tubes to control the flow of electricity. The vacuum tubes themselves ran only on electricity. They did not have moving parts. This made them faster and more reliable than the relays on the Mark computers. The UNIVAC read programs from magnetic tape. It was faster and sturdier than the paper tape used by the Mark computers.

THE FIRST COMPILER

While working on the UNIVAC I, Hopper noticed that the programmers were writing the same **code** over and over again. This caused them to redo work that someone else had already done. Hopper suggested they write their code one

The UNIVAC I filled an entire room. Scientists used it to perform calculations for physics research.

time and put it in a place where everyone else could find it. In notebooks and on loose sheets of paper, the programmers created a library of commonly used code. Hopper called these chunks of code **subroutines**.

The problem with those subroutines was that they had to be retyped into the computer each time someone wanted to use one. If a person made a typing mistake, the subroutine didn't work. Hopper thought it would be much easier if they could just type the subroutines into the computer once and let the computer store them.

Hopper served as director of systems research at Remington Rand, which bought out Eckert-Mauchly in 1950.

Hopper's team placed the subroutines on magnetic tape. The team assigned each subroutine a specific call number. Hopper then wrote a kind of code called a **compiler**. It told the computer how to find and use the subroutines. She dubbed the first compiler the A-0 System.

To use the compiler, a programmer typed in the call numbers of the subroutines he or she needed. The computer found the subroutines and performed the math. Before, a programmer might spend more than thirteen hours turning a mathematical equation into working code. With Hopper's compiler, the same task took only about forty-eight minutes.

Unfortunately, the A-0 did not catch on with other scientists. They didn't think computers could do the type of programming required of a compiler. However, Hopper's team continued to improve the compiler. When version A-2 was released, it was accepted by many people, including some scientists and government officials.

TECH TALK

"I had a running compiler and nobody would touch it. They told me computers could only do arithmetic."

—*Grace Hopper, discussing her first compiler*

17

Chapter 4

Hopper wanted to make the UNIVAC easier for customers to program.

COMPUTERS IN BUSINESS

After the success of the A-2 compiler, Hopper wanted to concentrate on other uses for computers. She believed they could also be used in business. For example, they could keep track of inventory in a warehouse, or they could send bills

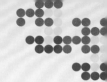

to customers. Plus, she wanted to make computers easier to use. Hopper felt that businesspeople should be able to write programs. She also believed they should be able to do so in English.

She wrote a new compiler called B-0. Instead of symbols, it used words such as *multiply* and *base-price*. To make her program more flexible, Hopper let programmers come up with their own words. For instance, if a mathematical equation had a **variable** in it, the programmer could name it *number of employees* or *number of hours worked*.

Another advantage of writing programs using English words was that it was easy for another programmer to understand

TECH TALK

"[I]t was Grace Hopper who helped teach the machines a language, stopped them from speaking in undecipherable numbers, enabled them to speak in English or French or German or whatever language you choose."

—*Television journalist Morley Safer, in a 1983 feature on Hopper*

what the first programmer wanted to do. All he or she had to do was read the code. Instead of individuals working on programs by themselves, teams could now work together. They could tackle more complicated problems. Plus, people with few computer skills could still understand the programs.

When the B-0 compiler-based programming language was released in 1958, the marketing department changed the name to FLOW-MATIC. Businesses such as US Steel and Westinghouse began using it for their payroll and inventory.

Westinghouse manufactured many types of electrical equipment, including shortwave radios.

The Ordnance Discrete Variable Automatic Computer (ORDVAC) was one of several new computers developed in the 1950s. Each used its own language.

DEVELOPING COBOL

The idea of creating business-friendly code was catching on. Other companies developed languages similar to FLOW-MATIC. But each language was linked to one particular computer, just as FLOW-MATIC was linked to the UNIVAC I. If a company wanted to change computers, they also had to change their computer language. This could be extremely expensive and time-consuming. Hopper and other programmers wanted to create a computer language that would be standard from company to company and from computer to computer.

In 1959, the Department of Defense had more than two hundred computers, and almost that many on order. Since their computers were from different manufacturers, they used different languages. The Department of Defense knew this would be expensive to maintain. So it established a committee to create a standard computer language.

The Department of Defense asked Hopper to serve on the committee. She insisted that English be used for the new language. As a result, FLOW-MATIC became the blueprint for the new language, which was called COBOL. This was short for Common Business-Oriented Language. Because of Hopper's role in its creation, she became known as the "Grandmother of COBOL."

COBOL was hugely successful. It could run on different computers for both businesses and the military. Because the Department of Defense used COBOL, any company that wanted to work with them had to use COBOL too. Within ten years, COBOL had become the most-used computer language in the world.

Hopper demonstrates the use of COBOL on a UNIVAC computer.

Chapter 5

A librarian prints a document on a UNIVAC printer in 1966. By then, the UNIVAC had evolved to serve more purposes.

A SHORT
RETIREMENT

By the mid-1960s, Hopper had established a successful career. As a senior staff scientist with UNIVAC, she was well known in the computer industry. She was a technical advisor to the Department of Defense. And she was involved

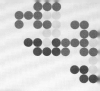

in installing computing systems for the navy. With her love of teaching, she was also a visiting professor at the University of Pennsylvania. In addition, she had achieved the rank of commander in the US Naval Reserve.

In 1966, at the age of fifty-nine, Hopper was forced to retire from the navy because of her age. But seven months later, the navy realized they had a problem. And they needed Hopper's help to solve it.

BACK ON ACTIVE DUTY

In 1967, the navy could not seem to develop a working payroll system on their computers. Over the years, different versions of COBOL had been developed. This caused problems.

Hopper's job was to standardize the navy's computers. She would make sure the same version of COBOL was being used on each one. At first, Hopper was asked to work on the project for six months. But Hopper worked for the navy for nineteen more years.

In 1985, Hopper was promoted to rear admiral. She was one of the first women to achieve that rank. In addition, she received numerous awards and honors. The navy even named a ship after her: the USS *Hopper.* When she retired again in 1986, the Department of Defense gave her the Defense

Hopper *(right)* shakes hands with President Ronald Reagan after her promotion to the rank of commodore in 1983.

Hopper *(fourth from left)* appears at the 1985 groundbreaking ceremonies for the Grace M. Hopper Navy Regional Data Automation Center in North Island, California.

Distinguished Service Medal. In 1991 she received the National Medal of Technology. This was the highest honor in the country for engineering and technology.

In 1992 Admiral Grace Hopper died at the age of eighty-five. She was buried in Arlington National Cemetery with full military honors. Hopper is considered a true pioneer in the computer field because of her work in creating COBOL, which remains a popular computer programming language. Her legacy lives on in the work of modern computer programmers, who still use many of the practices Hopper helped to create.

TIMELINE

1906

Grace Murray is born on December 9 in New York, New York.

1928

Grace Murray graduates from Vassar College.

1930

Murray marries Vincent Foster Hopper and changes her name to Grace Murray Hopper.

1934

Hopper earns a PhD in mathematics at Yale.

1943

Hopper joins the US Naval Reserve.

1944

Hopper begins working on the Mark I computer at Harvard University.

1949

Hopper joins Eckert-Mauchly as a senior mathematician to work on the UNIVAC I.

1959

COBOL is released.

1966

Hopper retires from the navy, but returns to active duty seven months later.

1992

Hopper dies at age eighty-five.

SOURCE NOTES

7   Walter Isaacson, "Grace Hopper, computing pioneer," *Harvard Gazette*, December 3, 2014, http://news.harvard.edu/gazette/story/2014/12/grace -hopper-computing-pioneer.

9   Ibid.

17 John H. Cushman, Jr., "Admiral Hopper's Farewell," *New York Times*, August 14, 1986, http://www.nytimes.com/1986/08/14/us/washington-talk-admiral -hopper-s-farewell.html.

19 "Grace Hopper: She Taught Computers to Talk," *60 Minutes Overtime*, December 9, 2013, http://www.cbsnews.com/news/grace-hopper-she -taught-computers-to-talk.

25 Kathleen Broom Williams, *Grace Hopper: Admiral of the Cyber Sea* (Annapolis, MD: Naval Institute Press, 2013), 85.

GLOSSARY

code
a system of letters, numbers, or symbols that convey information to a computer

compiler
a computer program that translates a set of instructions into a computer language so the computer can follow the instructions

debug
to find and remove errors in a computer program

program
instructions that a computer follows

subroutine
a program that performs a single task and that can be used repeatedly

variable
a piece of a mathematical equation that stands for a number

FURTHER INFORMATION

BOOKS

Bedell, Jane (J. M.). *So You Want to Be a Coder?* New York: Simon and Schuster, 2016. Learn about the different types of careers you can pursue if you write computer code.

Reed, Jennifer. *Computer Scientist Jean Bartik.* Minneapolis: Lerner Publications, 2017. Learn about Jean Bartik, another pioneering computer programmer.

Swaby, Rachel. *Trailblazers: 33 Women in Science Who Changed the World.* New York: Delacorte Books for Young Readers, 2016. Read about some of the most influential women in science.

WEBSITES

The Mark I Computer at Harvard University
http://chsi.harvard.edu/markone/index.html
Watch a video about the history of the Mark I computer.

Scratch
https://scratch.mit.edu
Learn basic computer programming skills and create your own interactive stories, games, and animations.

Women in Science and Technology
https://www.whitehouse.gov/women-in-stem
Listen to women who work in government talk about their heroes in science, technology, engineering, and math.

LERNER
e
SOURCE

Expand learning beyond the printed book. Download free, complementary educational resources for this book from our website, www.lerneresource.com.

INDEX

ABOUT THE AUTHOR

Andrea Pelleschi has been writing and editing children's books for over twelve years, including novels, storybooks, novelty books, graphic novels, and educational nonfiction books. She has a Master of Fine Arts degree in creative writing from Emerson College and has taught writing classes for college freshmen. She currently lives in Cincinnati, Ohio.